*Wishing you
many blessings*

To

From

Blessings

When I first open my eyes
upon the morning meadows and
look out upon the beautiful
world, I thank God I am alive.

RALPH WALDO EMERSON

Step boldly into the future as you dream it, for without great risks there can be no great rewards.

The true harvest of my daily life is somewhat intangible and indescribable as the tints of morning or evening. It is a little star dust caught, a segment of the rainbow which I have clutched.

HENRY DAVID THOREAU

It is only when men begin to worship that they begin to grow.

CALVIN COOLIDGE

Happiness and sadness are emotions that are within our power of choice. The decision is made inside the heart.

I celebrate the gift of contentment, knowing there is no guarantee it will last. But for now, it's great to rest—just to rest—in this wonderful calm.

Happiness is contagious! If allowed to spread,

it can infect the whole universe with joy.

The hug of sunlight, the smell of rain, the soft touch of snowflakes, and the comforting crunch of leaves beneath our feet are nature's callings to come and play!

If we had no winter,

the spring would not be

so pleasant.

ANNE BRADSTREET

When I'm bored, remind me: This is the excitement of life—darkness alternating with light, down dancing with up—and inactivity is absolutely essential, as a prelude, to the most fulfilling experiences of all.

When feeling inadequate or overwhelmed, consider that the forest
would be silent if the birds sang only the songs they had perfected.

When broken dreams
cross my path, it helps to
know that it takes broken soil
to grow a flower, broken
clouds to bring rain, and
broken grain to
make bread.

A successful person doesn't quit trying once a goal is reached,

but sets a new one and keeps going.

If you find stumbling blocks in your path,

use them as stepping stones to move

closer to the good in life.

There's no such thing
as an average day.
Each one is unique,
unlike any other,
and will happen only
once in the entire history
of the universe.

Think of each day
as a special gift and
unwrap it gratefully.

A small lantern that sheds only enough light for the next step may still illuminate the entire journey, one step at a time.

Our smiles reflect the joy within us.

Perhaps if we smile more often,

others will behold God in us and

find joy in our happiness.

It isn't the great big pleasures that count the most;

it's making a great deal out of the little ones.

JEAN WEBSTER

A small thing, as simple as a breath of fresh air, supports the changes
we make: The present is breathing in and the past is exhalation.

Some say it's wrong to live in the past, but in truth,

the present moves so quickly that the past is all we have.

Plan a future that will become a past worth having.

A kind and compassionate act is often its own reward.

If you have something to do,

someone to love,

and something to hope for,

every day becomes a celebration.

All it takes to triumph over adversity is the conviction that you can.

Beginning each day as if something good will happen moves us further toward that possibility. Doubt, however, seldom takes the first step.

Of all the good gifts that the

　　Lord lets fall,

Is not silence the best of all?

The deep, sweet hush when the

　　song is closed,

And every sound but a voiceless ghost;

And every sigh, as we listening leant,

A breathless quiet of vast content?

The laughs we laughed have a

　　purer ring

With but their memory echoing;

So of all the good gifts the

　　Lord lets fall,

Is not silence the best of all?

JAMES WHITCOMB RILEY, "BEST OF ALL"

Recognize that not all being-alone is loneliness, and not all solitude is a problem to solve. Rejoice in the blessing of quietness.

So much to celebrate!
Waking to dawn gilding trees;

squeezing fresh orange juice,
its zest clinging to my hands
all day; making a new friend,
talking to an old one;

watching the first leaf bud, raking the last.

Each day's turning brings gifts to celebrate.

If you've forgotten what joy looks like, watch a child chasing soap bubbles for the first time.

Celebrate love. It is the breath of your existence,
and the best of all reasons for living.

I gain strength, courage, and confidence by every experience in which I must stop and look fear in the face.

ELEANOR ROOSEVELT

If you only keep your eyes on the path before you, you won't get lost, but neither will you see the stars.

Cultivate enthusiasm,
for it brings new life into
old tasks and humor and joy
into dull situations.

To those who believe we live in a world of sorrow,

offer the gifts of joy and laughter.

The little cares that fretted me,

I lost them yesterday,

Among the fields above the sea,

Among the winds at play, . . .

Among the hushing of the corn,

Where drowsy poppies nod,

Where ill thoughts die and good are born–

Out in the fields of God.

ANONYMOUS, *OUT IN THE FIELDS*

A kind heart is a
fountain of gladness,
making everything
in its vicinity
freshen into smiles.

WASHINGTON IRVING

Birds begin
singing again
before the storm
has fully ended,
having known all
along that clouds
cover, not
banish, the sun.

It is good to know that adversity makes one wise,
though perhaps not rich. In great attempts at success,
it is glorious even to fail.

You'll know your life is blessed when the worst problem you have is
that the birds outside your window are singing too loudly.

Trust the call of
the future with
the same spirit
as the bird who
sings to greet
the dawn while
it is still dark.

Celebrate your

spontaneity.

Enjoy all of creation,

each leaf and flower and every small pebble along the way.

Embrace the hope of each new morning,

and the last ray of sunshine to fall at day's end.

It matters not
how long you live,
but how well.

PUBLILIUS SYRUS

There is pleasure in new
friendships, comfort in old
ones, and sweet memories to
treasure in those we've lost.

Link your roots deeply into whatever task you are doing,
for commitment and enthusiasm transform monotony into
freshness and routine into joy and discovery.

A positive attitude
helps bridge the gap
between ability and
expectations.

Don't seek peace and tranquility from outside sources;

they are hidden inside your own heart.

When poised at the brink of new beginnings, you can either find a ladder to climb or learn to fly.

Go in peace.

You are not alone in the world.

Rejoice in friendships, fellowships,

acquaintances, parties, and

get-togethers of every kind.

You are not alone.

Rejoice.

Shadows fall out of sight when eyes are raised to the sun in optimism.

Life, like a river
on its way to
the sea,
is fed and
joined by small
streams of love
and kindness
so that it
grows fuller
and stronger
on the way.

Seek comfort in the garden,

seek adventure on the mountain,

but seek the truth within yourself.

To find joy and fulfillment, it is only necessary to trust your heart.

Like mile
markers on a map,
memories connect
me to my past and
guide me to the
future.